THE BABY AND THE SEED

A Primer on Good Parenting

A Book for the Entire Family

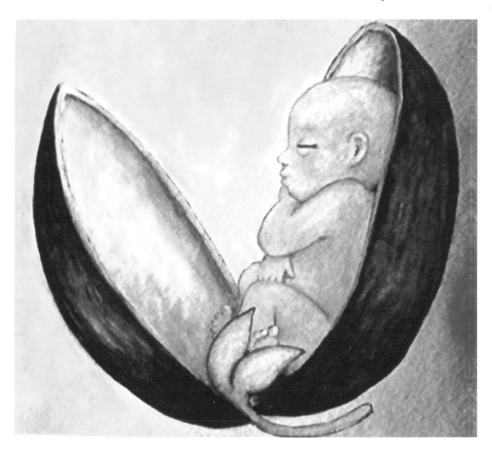

Leland "Bud" Beamer, MD

Illustrations

Kirk Charlton

Portraits by Paul Lanquist

To order additional copies of this book, contact:
Xlibris
844-714-8691
www.Xlibris.com
Orders@Xlibris.com

ISBN: 978-1-6641-2463-9 (sc)
ISBN: 978-1-6641-2462-2 (hc)
ISBN: 978-1-6641-2464-6 (e)

Library of Congress Control Number: 2020915622

Print information available on the last page

Rev. date: 08/20/2020

To my dear mother Elizabeth Evans Beamer.

To Kirk Charlton's daughter, Sophie.

To the many incarcerated men and women who suffered from abuse, neglect, and significant family dysfunction in their critical formative years.

To Hana Hooper, a beautiful young lady who withstood strokes, blindness, and a heart transplant and demonstrated courage and resilience beyond our imagination.

It is hard to straighten in the oak the crook
that formed in the sapling.
—A Gaelic saying

Introduction

This book is written for everyone. It is an attempt to help educate all of us so that we may have a better understanding of why we become who we are and the importance of good parenting, particularly in the first few years of life.

Ninety-five percent of the brain develops in this critical period, and connections are formed that determine how we relate to one another and how we regulate our emotions as well as our center for learning. We now know that certain neurochemicals and hormones created by a stressful environment will rob us of these critical connecting pathways. We also know that a stressed brain has significant difficulty processing new information.

We all vary somewhat in our parenting skills, skills that were significantly influenced by how our parents raised us. Our ability to parent effectively is also challenged by the stresses of everyday life, be they financial issues, time constraints, societal factors, or problems created by not making the best of choices.

Parenting is the most important role we will ever have in our lives. It is not an easy role, and often, support in many forms is needed. It is OK to ask for help, for both parent and infant.

The architecture of our infants' brains is structured according to how we relate with them, day-to-day, moment to moment. The environment that our children live in will determine how their genes are expressed. Infants become a reflection of their environment.

Every effort needs to be made to reduce stress in the home. A healthy, safe, loving environment in the months of pregnancy and the first two years of life is of utmost importance in this stage of brain development when the core of an individual's ability to think, feel, and relate to others is formed.

If we are to prevent chronic disease conditions, mental, behavioral, and addiction disorders, as well as significant learning disabilities, parents need to understand the relationship of a caring environment and their baby's brain development. Dysfunction in this critical period is the basis for the multitude of these disorders later in life.

This book is centered on the poem "The Baby and the Seed," which is an illustrated poem that relates to the importance of nurturing on those things that we raise, be they human, animal, or plant.

The poem "Hungry Eyes" is included to introduce the importance of parents connecting with their baby as well as the nature of this critical connection.

We have also added an appendix to further emphasize the importance of love and resilience, as well as an illustrated section on how stress affects the structure of the infant's brain.

Hopefully, we can all continue to learn from one another, with our children's interests and development our highest priority.

Hungry Eyes

Their hungry eyes look and search
for a face that looks at them
looking back.

Eyes connect, and a soul is filled with a surge
of warmth and excitement unmatched by food
or other comforts.

If only each and every baby would find this source
of caring eyes and a face that smiles
and a voice that sings.

Would not her face be full of smiles
and her precious mind thrive and grow
to do good things.

The mind of a parent whose mind is preoccupied
may not truly see this baby or
be received in such a way.

And losing this opportunity, a baby's life is changed
and who she was to be is but a ghost
that follows her now lesser life.

There is that critical time when hungry eyes
and growing minds will reflect and thrive
and then this time will cease.

Let us be aware and let us care to act and support
and advocate for those who have no voice
and whose life in some way will affect us all.

*It should be a baby's right to be held
and loved and nurtured.*

The Baby and the Seed

A baby and a small wheat seed
have a lot in common, as you will see.
From their very beginnings, each needs much care.
Their needs are great so be aware.

It's not just planting the seed and standing by
or tending the baby just when she cries.
It is moment to moment every day,
knowing what matters in important ways.

Even the animals out on the farm
certainly need to be kept from harm.
But they also need loving care,
the nuzzling and licking of their bristly hair.

Good soil is needed for the seed to grow.
You plow and till and then harrow.
The seed will grow and wheat will come,
but first the water and the sun.

The baby, too, needs a good start,
a happy home, and a lot of heart.
Eyes connect and smiles are shared;
a parent and child are a loving pair.

Weeks go by and both will grow.

The ripened wheat will be cut and sold.

But baby still has many years.

There will be joy to share as well as tears.

For like the wheat with drought and weeds
and storms and wind and unmet needs,
the baby, too, will have hard days
when challenges come in many ways.

Unlike the wheat that grows without feelings,
baby needs to feel safe as growth is occurring.
As her brain grows and her body forms,
holding her close helps her deal with the storms.

Families also have challenging times
when Mommy gets sad and hard to find.
Fun and jobs may not be there;
as stress increases, there is need for care.

We cannot hold back the laws of nature
when storms and droughts put our crops in danger.
But in our homes where babies grow and stress deprives,
Love turns back the storms, and we can thrive.

So farmers and parents have similar roles,
raising babies or grains or calves or foals.
It takes nurturing care for all to succeed.
Good wheat and babies the world does need.

We must think of these things as a child grows,
or as a farmer, the seeds that he sows.
The people and wheat that they become
determined by care when they were young.

Appendix

Development of Emotions and Skills

Children will learn to love if they are loved,
and in play, they can practice this gift of love.
Playing with pets or dolls, they can learn to be kind.
Holding, eyes connecting, warm feelings they'll find.

So teach your children in everyday play
how to talk to their dolls in a nurturing way.
Or if it's a pet and they show gentle ways,
kindness will show in their later days.

Reading

To read to your child is a marvelous gift.
Bonds will form and spirits will lift.
Reading success and imagination thrive.
Hopes and big dreams are kept alive.

Music

Music, too, will bring great joy.
Many words and sounds to learn and enjoy.
Body and mind will work together.
Brain growth accelerates as skills get better.

Playing

Real life and relationships will help children grow.
They won't learn love and fairness from a screen or a show.
Laughing together or sharing a game,
watching a screen is not the same.

Kids, as they grow, need to have fun.
Their well-being will determine who they become.
To laugh, to relate, to imagine, and to create,
early play is important, so don't hesitate.

Sharing Chores

Getting children involved in everyday chores
will make the most of everyday hours.
Talk to them as you fold the clothes,
or engage them as you paint your toes.

Caring

Like a plant, our children will continue to grow,
and joy will be determined by the love that we show.
When it's all said and done and our work is through,
have they learned from us what caring can do?

Resilience

Science has sought to strengthen the wheat
to resist the winds, the drought, and the heat.
As the child grows, she will stumble and fall.
Love and support will help her stand tall.

It is important to have that someone who cares.
Difficult times will be easier to bear.
Kindness and support directed their way
will give children the strength to face each day.

Love

Love is so much more than just saying I love you.
It is a shoulder to cry on when you are blue.
It is spending the time with you to laugh and play
and tucking you in at the end of the day.

You will continue to grow like the planted seed,
and I must be careful as you follow me.
My love will show in the things that I do.
I will do right because I care for you.

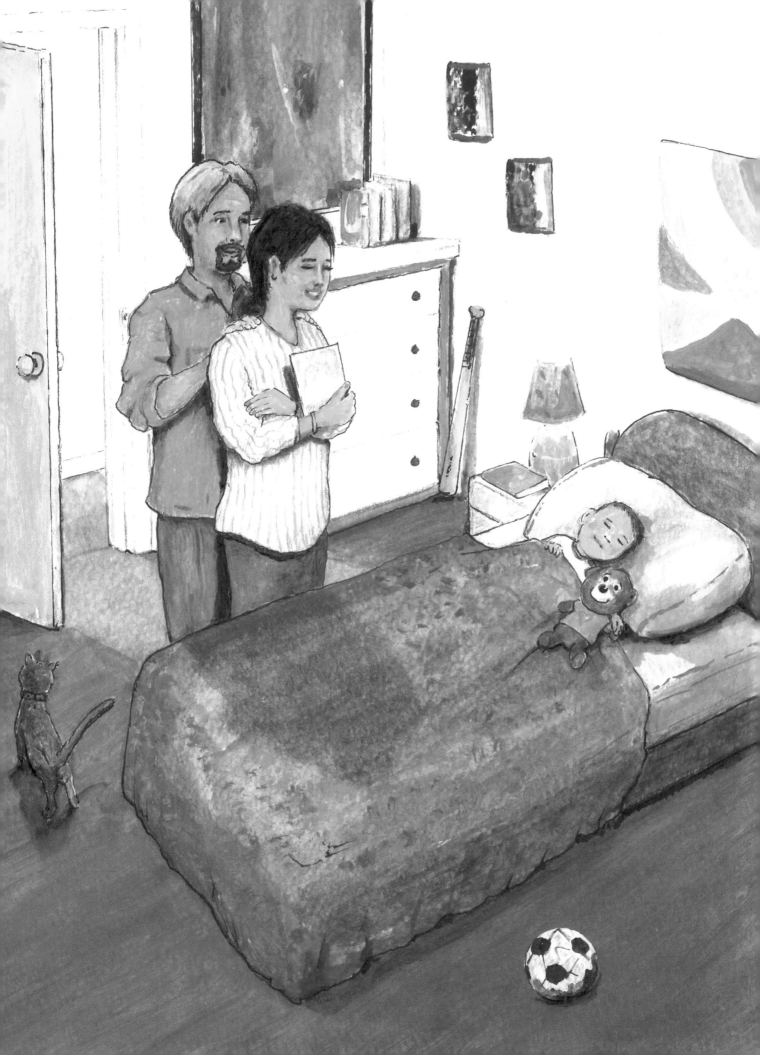

Illustrations

The Effects of Stress on the Growing Brain

Toxic stress in the home causes the release of a neurochemical (norepinephrine) and a stress hormone (cortisol) that results in the loss of millions, if not billions, of brain pathways that are critical for brain function.

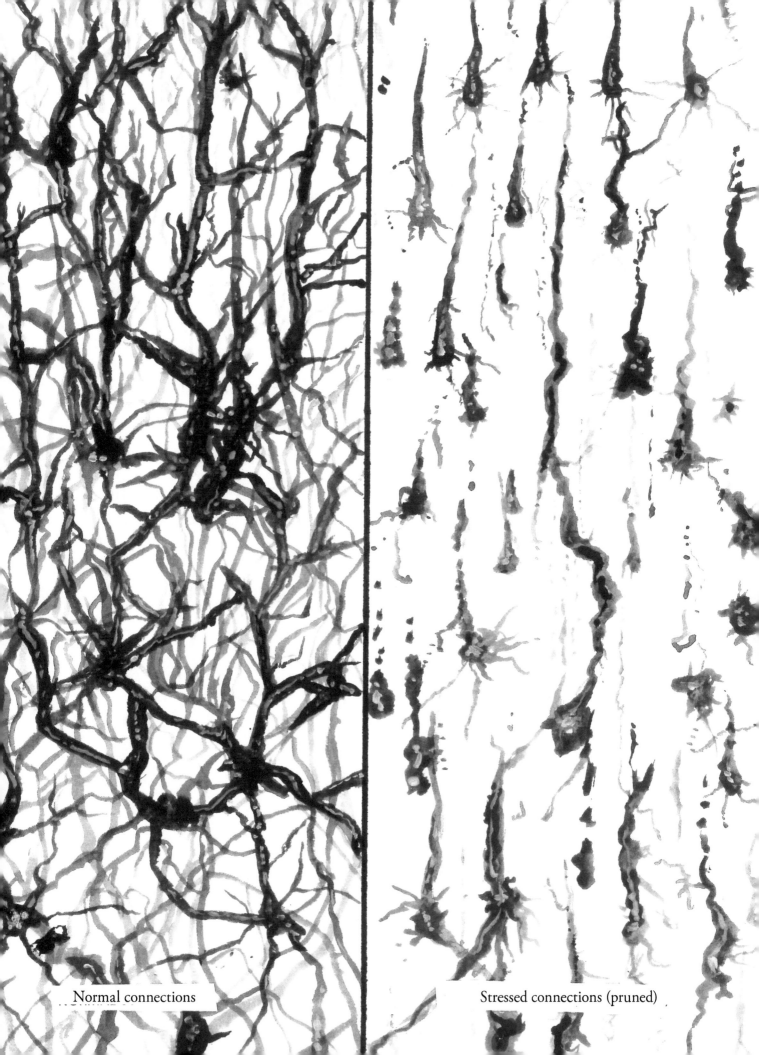

Normal connections

Stressed connections (pruned)

Pathways for compassion for others (empathy) and self-regulation, which is critical for learning and coping with stress, are extremely sensitive to chemicals created by toxic stress. These connections are damaged and destroyed and, as a result, are pruned from the brain.

In addition, in some areas of the brain, pathways for positive development are replaced by pathways for "red alert" and hyperreactivity.

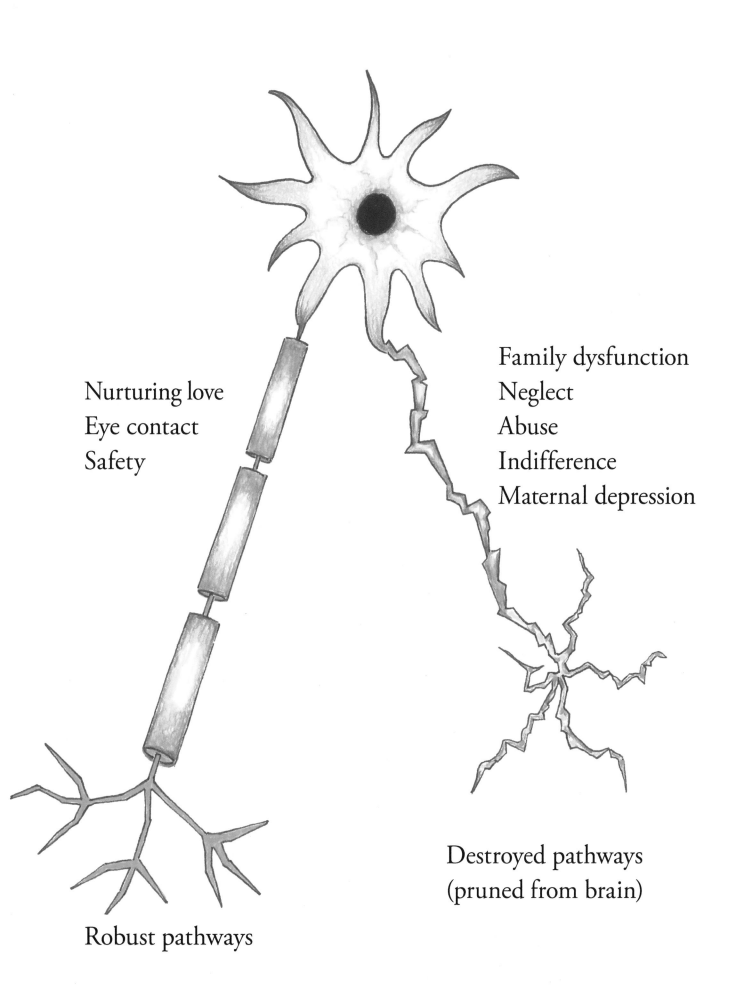

Nurturing love
Eye contact
Safety

Family dysfunction
Neglect
Abuse
Indifference
Maternal depression

Destroyed pathways
(pruned from brain)

Robust pathways

Connecting face-to-face and eyes to eyes is critical in a nurturing relationship.

When an adult responds to baby's gestures, babbles, and cries with her own eye contact, jabber, smiles, and loving words, mirror cells behind the eyes are activated and strengthened and build pathways to centers for empathy and learning and self-regulation.

This serve-and-return relationship is the foundation for baby's future behavior, development, and health.

Limbic center
(empathy)

Executive center
(learning and self-regulation)

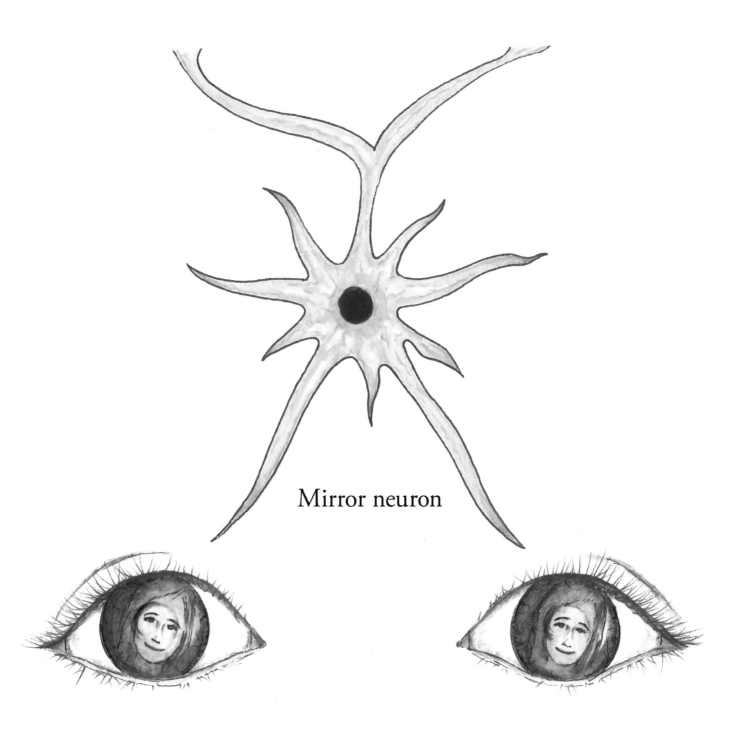

Mirror neuron

Adversity and Resilience

Tough times happen in all families. Always comfort your child and bring him or her back to baseline. This helps eliminate the toxic stress chemicals that have formed in the body. Consoling your child confirms that you truly care.

Some children fulfill our goals and some may not. Children need to know that they are loved even though they may not live up to our expectations. We must love them unconditionally.

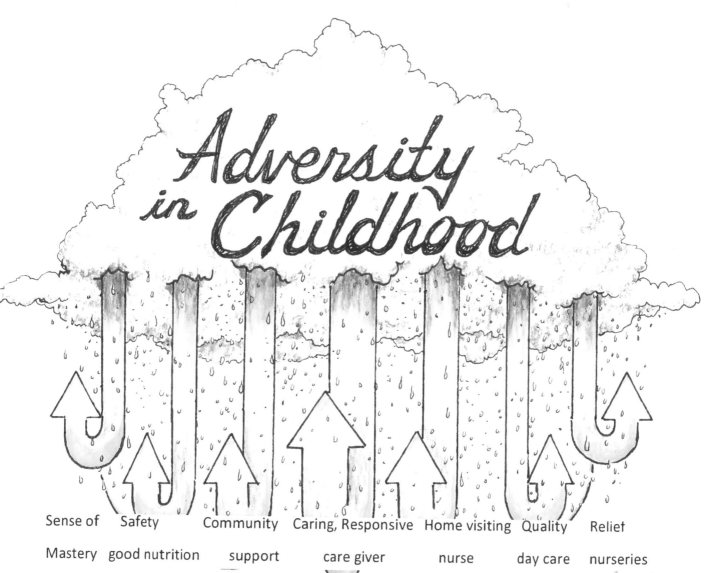

Sense of   Safety   Community   Caring, Responsive   Home visiting   Quality   Relief

Mastery good nutrition   support   care giver   nurse   day care   nurseries

Resources

Sometimes we need help and be taught what to do. Parenting can be difficult for me and for you. There is help out there in many forms. Turn to resources before and after baby is born.

1. Discuss with medical provider if you need help.
2. Nurse home visitation: everyone, regardless of circumstances, can benefit from this service at this most crucial time.
3. Vroom.org: a phone app that will provide daily tips for parent/child interaction that helps brain development and the building of stronger relationships.
4. Early Head Start: provides and supports early education and family relationships.
5. Relief Nurseries: provide therapeutic intervention and mentored child-to-child interaction
6. Google "getting help in early childhood" for literature resources.

Closing

*For the thousands beating at the leaves of
evil, there is one striking at the root.*
— Thoreau

Let us work together and get to the cause of the
problems and prevent the disorders created by a stressful
childhood.

It is never too early to start attachment and connecting
with your baby. *Love is magic!* It can create a caring,
healthy, capable human being that becomes a contributing
member of society.

Background and References

Gabor Mate, MD, author of *In the Realm of Hungry Ghosts*, who proposed the metaphor of the needs of a seed of wheat and that of a baby.

Bruce Perry, MD, PhD, whose works and lectures have led the way in helping us understand the impact of emotional brain trauma in early childhood.

T. Berry Brazelton, MD, for the values, principles, and practices that helped guide us.

Center on the Developing Child, Harvard University, for the studies and research pertaining to brain architecture and the impact of serve and return.

Ghosts from the Nursery by Karr-Morse and Wiley, a poignant study on the effects of toxic stress on the neurobiology of the brain.

Nadine Burke Harris, MD, a California surgeon general, for her TED talks and book *The Deepest Well: Healing Long Term Effects of Childhood Adversity*.

"The Lifelong Effects of Early Childhood Adversity and Toxic Stress," *Pediatrics*, vol. 121 (December 26, 2011).

Beth Ann Aeschliman Beamer, RN, my wife—a public health nurse who works with young families—for her patience, advice, and wisdom.

Leland "Bud" Beamer, MD, is a native of Iowa where he attended Cornell College and the University of Iowa (Carver) College of Medicine. After nearly forty years of serving his community in Madras, Oregon, as a family doctor and surgeon, he is now chief medical officer at a state prison near Madras. His interest in the early childhood period and why we become who we are has intensified while working with the adults in incarceration and understanding their early beginnings.

He authored the book *A River: The Thread that Binds*, which is a collection of poems and essays related to fishing, rivers, life, and family.

Kirk Charlton is an artist who has turned his life around after serving time behind prison walls. He has dedicated his life and career to helping others through his work of art. His popular children's book series I Wannabe includes such books as *I Want to Be an Archaeologist* and *I Want to Be a Marine Biologist*. He has also developed a program called Art Inside Out for incarcerated individuals who uses art to help individuals heal and restore their value.

Paul Lanquist is a popular commercial artist whose works are in venues throughout the northwest.

About the Book

This is a book for everyone. In using the metaphor comparing the raising of the seed of wheat with that of a baby, the importance of a nurturing environment is presented. Using a poem for structure, accompanied by colorful illustrations that convey the message in each stanza, we can better understand the significance of a good start in life.

Knowing that 90 percent of the brain develops in the months of pregnancy and the first two years of life and that most chronic medical, behavioral, and addiction disorders occur in adults who had dysfunction in this critical period makes it imperative that every effort be made to educate us all on the importance of good responsive parenting.

It is the attempt of this book to contribute to this greater understanding. Illustrations demonstrating the effects of toxic stress on the brain and sections relating specifically to love, adversity, and resilience have been added because of the impact they have on why we become who we are.

CPSIA information can be obtained
at www.ICGtesting.com
Printed in the USA
BVHW020042240221
600892BV00020B/268